Dr Katrina Warren is a veteri
television screens in 1994 as a ļ

MW01145250

Totally Wild. She then went on to co-host the hit TV show *Harry's Practice*, and became a household name for promoting responsible pet ownership and animal welfare. She has worked extensively in Australia and the USA on television and radio, and has written for the print media and the internet. Katrina has written three books, regularly MCs events and does dog training talks and demonstrations.

Katrina loves all animals but has a huge passion for Border Collies – particularly chocolate ones. Her beloved Border Collie, Toby, won hearts across the country for his mischievous personality and amazing repertoire of tricks, which resulted in the original best-selling book, *Wonderdog*.

Kelly Gill has over 19 years' experience as a veterinary nurse and dog trainer. She competes with her dogs in Obedience, Agility and Heelwork to Music, and has over 100 Obedience and Agility titles – twice achieving the top title of Australian Obedience Champion. She enjoys the challenges of training dogs to have fun in obedience competitions, and of working with dogs and cats for the film industry, and performing tricks on stage with her team of very talented chocolate and white Border Collies. Kelly has been breeding Border Collies since 1999 under the KERODAN prefix and is lucky enough to live on a large property in the Hunter Valley with her partner Robert, family of nine Border Collies, a Pug, two cats and a miniature pony.

WONDERDOGS

TRICKS AND TRAINING

DR KATRINA WARREN
AND KELLY GILL

HarperCollins*Publishers*

This book is dedicated to the memory of my best friend and loyal companion, Toby — my shining light who filled my life with fun and unconditional love.
Missed every day and loved forever.

x

CONTENTS

INTRODUCTION

In 2001, my first book, *Wonderdog*, was published, featuring my chocolate Border Collie, Toby. Famous for his appearances on the television show *Harry's Practice*, Toby was admired by pet lovers across the country. A born entertainer, Toby loved to perform to a crowd and brought smiles to the faces of everyone he met. He inspired people to have fun with their dogs and enhance the relationship they shared with them.

Sadly, Toby passed away in 2010. I miss him terribly, but I am delighted that his legacy lives on in this new book, *Wonderdogs: Tricks and Training*.

I have had the pleasure of working with Kelly Gill and her team of beautiful Border Collies for several years now. Kelly is passionate about helping owners to find joy in training their pets without the use of force. Her techniques are based on positive reinforcement with lots of rewards. She finds sheer enjoyment in working out how to challenge dogs and cats to view training as a game. The Wonderdogs are a demonstration of this. They are confident, motivated, happy dogs who have fun, even in the most challenging circumstances and environments, whether it be competing or performing complex tricks for captivated audiences.

Kelly and I have worked very closely to create a book suitable for dogs of all ages, from puppies through to adults. The way in which you manage and train your puppy from the start will have a huge influence on his behaviour as an adult dog, so we have included some management strategies to set your puppy up for life. All dogs enjoy the challenge of learning new tricks, and adult dogs are no exception. We have included fun tricks to teach puppies and adult dogs alike, proving no dog is too old to learn.

At the time of writing, I had recently adopted a beautiful Golden Retriever named Riley from a wonderful organisation, Golden Retriever Rescue. Riley was found starving, flea-ridden, and with horribly infected wounds on all his legs. He really needed help, physically and emotionally, so I offered to foster him. He never moved out!

Dr Katrina and Riley

It has given me enormous satisfaction to nurse Riley back to health and see a new sparkle in his eyes. He is a happy family pet who makes friends wherever he goes. I am conscious, however, that he lacks confidence in certain situations because he was probably not well socialised as a pup. My priority will always be to not place him in situations that he finds stressful.

Riley had no house manners when I met him but he is testament that with the right motivation, you can train an adult dog. Riley *loves* food, so using treats as a reward, we have already perfected his basic commands such as **SIT**, **STAY** and **DROP** around the home. Much to my daughter's delight, he has also started learning tricks, such as **SHAKE HANDS** and **SPIN**.

Teaching our dogs tricks allows us to have fun with them and it enhances our relationship with them. We hope this book will further develop your special bond with your dog, and allow you to create your very own Wonderdog.

MEET THE WONDERDOGS

Jinx   Flynn   Tigger   Willow   Jordie

WILLOW

DOB 28/4/99

NICKNAMES Willy, Woo Woo, The Queen.

FAMILY I'm the oldest member of the team, the mother of Jinx and Jordie. Grandmother to Flynn.

GREATEST ACHIEVEMENTS I'm an Obedience champion and have all my Agility titles. I've had three beautiful litters of puppies. I've done loads of TV work and stage shows.

FAVOURITE TRICK TAKE A BOW.

FAVOURITE HOBBIES Sleeping on Kelly's bed at night. I also love to perform on stage.

OBSESSIONS Watching swallows play and nose bopping people.

NAUGHTIEST DEED Stealing a whole roast chicken from the kitchen bench.

PET HATES Having my nails clipped, being left at home when the others go out and being told I'm a dog!

KNOWN ACCOMPLICE Jordie.

JORDIE

DOB 12/11/02
NICKNAMES Jords, Do Do, Dooey, Smartypants.
FAMILY My Mum is the amazing Willow, I'm a half-sister to Jinx, and Mum to the very handsome Flynn.
GREATEST ACHIEVEMENTS I have lots of Agility and Obedience titles. Then there are heaps of TV commercials and loads of stage show performances. Oh, and having my two beautiful litters of puppies.
FAVOURITE TRICK This is hard, as I'm a true show-off, but probably SIT PRETTY. It gets the most attention, but I'm prepared to do whatever it takes!
FAVOURITE HOBBIES I have a lot of these! Let's see, being the centre of attention, making people laugh. Lying on my back in someone's lap. Eating food, especially any treats.
OBSESSIONS Being in front of the camera, and I love the vacuum cleaner, it's way too much fun.
NAUGHTIEST DEED Pulling the cat off the kitchen bench when he was looking at some food.
PET HATES Someone else in front of the camera and being told I'm wrong.
KNOWN ACCOMPLICE Willow.

JINX

DOB 3/7/06
NICKNAMES Stinky, Dinky.
FAMILY My Mum is the amazing Willow, I'm a half-sister to Jordie.
GREATEST ACHIEVEMENTS I have lots of Agility and Obedience titles, two beautiful litters of puppies, and I keep the magpies out of the yard – a very important job. Then of course there's all the stage shows I do too.

FAVOURITE TRICK SPEAKING. I love the sound of my own voice!
FAVOURITE HOBBIES My tug rope, the chuck-it, any toy really. Diving into the dam.
OBSESSIONS Nibbling on people's buttons and chasing magpies.
NAUGHTIEST DEED Chasing the pony.
PET HATES Without a doubt, being bathed! And watching someone else performing with Kelly.
KNOWN ACCOMPLICE Flynn.

FLYNN

DOB 18/02/08

NICKNAMES Mister Man, Flynny.

FAMILY My Mum is Jordie and my Grandma is the amazing Willow.

GREATEST ACHIEVEMENTS I have lots of Agility and Obedience titles. I performed in my very first TV commercial at 10 weeks old, and I was a little star: it's in my genes. Now I have heaps of TV stuff and stage show performances, and I am flown all over Australia.

FAVOURITE TRICKS SPINS, LEG WEAVE and giving pretty ladies flowers.

FAVOURITE HOBBIES I am a real ladies' man and know how to win hearts with my dashing good looks and charisma. I love swimming, my ball on a rope, the chuck-it, the sport agility, and I especially love sleeping upside down on the lounge and hanging out with the pony.

OBSESSIONS Tigger the cat and agility.

NAUGHTIEST DEED Digging the biggest hole.

PET HATES Getting into trouble and being kept up past my bedtime.

KNOWN ACCOMPLICE Tigger the cat.

TIGGER (Honorary Wonderdog)

BORN 2009
NICKNAME Tiggie.
FAMILY I'm a rags-to-riches story. I was rescued from a pound just as my time was up. Kelly took one look at me and immediately knew I had what it would take to be in the film industry. The rest is history as I now live with the Wonderdogs and Kelly.
GREATEST ACHIEVEMENTS Getting out of the pound! I've done lots of stage shows and even a few TV commercials.
FAVOURITE TRICK Touching or sitting up on anything I'm asked to.
FAVOURITE HOBBIES I just have to be in all photos. Hanging out with the Wonderdogs and being involved in the computer work by sitting on the keyboard. I love to go out in the car, meet people and be admired on stage too.
OBSESSIONS Knocking anything off benches with my paws.
NAUGHTIEST DEED Jumping into photos unannounced.
PET HATES Being bathed! Being left at home when the dogs go out and being told I'm a cat.
KNOWN ACCOMPLICE Flynn.

PART 1

PUPPIES

Welcoming a new puppy into your family is a really exciting time. Puppies are adorable and fun but they are also energetic, mischievous and time-consuming.

The first few months of your pup's life are extremely important to his development, and how you manage your puppy during this time will greatly influence his happiness and behaviour as an adult dog. Your puppy needs to learn to socialise properly with people, dogs and other animals. He also needs to learn house rules, good manners and basic obedience.

Having a strategy to help integrate your new puppy into the family will ensure a rewarding and positive experience for everyone and build a lifelong bond between you and your dog.

PUPPY CARE

Clair

Vaccinations

Puppies need three vaccinations to protect them against Parvovirus, Distemper, Hepatitis and Canine Cough.

Vaccinate at 6 to 8 weeks, 12 weeks and 16 weeks.

Intestinal worms

Puppies can be infected with worms before they are born or through their mother's milk. They also pick them up from dog faeces. Puppies should be wormed regularly for roundworm, hookworm, tapeworm and whipworm.

Worm at 2, 4, 8, and 12 weeks and then at 4 months, 5 months, and 6 months.

Then worm every 3 months for life.

Heartworm

Heartworm disease is caused by a parasite that is transmitted by mosquitoes. Adult worms clog the heart, leading to heart disease and death if untreated.

Start heartworm protection by 12 weeks of age.

Dogs older than 6 months need a blood test before starting treatment.

Options include a monthly tablet, monthly spot-on (where you squeeze the solution directly onto the skin) or annual injection.

Fleas

Fleas are a terrible nuisance and can cause an aggravating skin condition called flea allergy dermatitis. Left uncontrolled, fleas can quickly breed to create an unwelcome infestation in your home (a breeding pair of fleas could produce more than 20,000 fleas in 3 months). There are several options for flea control including tablets and spot-on products that provide monthly protection.

Desexing

Puppies should be desexed by around 6 months of age. Unless you have reason to breed from your dog, you should have it desexed to avoid unwanted pregnancies. Desexing decreases the risk of mammary cancer in female dogs and prostate cancer in male dogs.

Desexed dogs are less likely to roam.

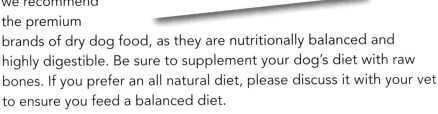

Pearl

Archie

Diet

There is a huge variety of commercial food on the market and we recommend the premium brands of dry dog food, as they are nutritionally balanced and highly digestible. Be sure to supplement your dog's diet with raw bones. If you prefer an all natural diet, please discuss it with your vet to ensure you feed a balanced diet.

Archie

Dental care

Gum disease is very common in dogs so regular attention should be given to dental care. Some hard dry food should be included in your dog's diet as this will help clean the teeth and gums. Fresh marrowbones, once or twice a week, also help. You can also teach your dog to have his teeth brushed regularly. This is best taught from puppyhood.

Grooming

All dogs require some level of grooming depending on their breed and coat type. Get your puppy used to the basics and brush his coat regularly with a soft brush, paying special attention to the ears, belly and tail. Get your puppy used to regular bathing too. If your pup is going to require clipping, it's a good idea to expose him early to the sights and sounds of a grooming salon.

Dusty

Nails

A dog's nails continue to grow and unless he is pounding the pavements daily, it is probable they will need regular trimming. The key is to cut only the tip of the nail, avoiding the blood vessel inside (called the quick). You can see the quick inside light-coloured nails, but cannot see it in dark nails.

Risk

Handling

I cannot emphasise enough how important it is to handle your puppy daily and get him used to being touched all over and held by you. Touch and handle his paws, tail and ears, and get the puppy used to having his mouth opened and his tail lifted. Reassure and reward constantly and your puppy will learn that being touched is pleasant.

Identification

You must register your puppy with your local council and many councils also require that your pet is microchipped.

Ask your vet to microchip your pup, if it hasn't already been done. This will identify your puppy for life and details are recorded on a database that will be used to reunite you both in the event that your pup gets lost. Remember to update your details if you change address.

It is also important to make sure your puppy is wearing an identification tag which includes your pup's name and your phone number. This is the simplest and quickest way to be reunited with your puppy if he escapes or gets lost.

Archie

Pearl

CHILDREN AND PUPPIES

There is something truly magical about the bond shared between children and puppies. It can be a wonderful experience for a child to grow up with a family dog but it is important that you are sensible in your approach when you introduce a puppy. This is important for the safety of your child and of your pup.

Prior to bringing home a puppy, discuss with your children some basic ground rules that the whole family must agree to. Read some easy books about puppy care and ask your children to answer basic questions about looking after a pup.

Toddlers are particularly difficult because you cannot reason with them. They are unpredictable and often treat puppies like a toy. Ideally, wait until your child is at least five years old before welcoming a puppy. If you do have a toddler and a puppy, you must actively supervise (staying within an arm's length) or separate them.

Provide your puppy with a safe haven, a warm area that is out of bounds to children and gives your puppy the comfort of bedding, toys, food and water bowls. A puppy playpen is the best option for this (see page 24).

Lisa with puppy Zing

Supervision is essential. Never leave a young child unsupervised with a puppy. Children can easily hurt puppies by poking them, pulling on their tail or standing on them. A puppy has razor-sharp teeth and can easily nip or scratch a child.

Children should sit on the ground to pat their pup. They should be taught to be calm and gentle around their puppy as squealing, stomping and loud activities may frighten a puppy. Don't allow rough play or chasing games as these types of activities will excite your pup, increasing the chance of nipping and jumping up.

Children should be taught to leave their puppy alone if he is sleeping, eating or in his puppy playpen. After playing with the puppy, children should be encouraged to wash their hands.

It is natural for a puppy to explore things (including little hands) with his mouth and most pups will jump up when excited until taught an alternative behaviour. Please read the sections on PLAY-BITING (page 34) and JUMPING UP (page 36).

Enrolling your puppy in puppy classes is important for his socialisation. It's also a great opportunity for children to learn about their puppy's needs and understand that puppies also go to school.

Dougal

SOCIALISATION

The first 18 weeks of age is the most important developmental period in your dog's life. This is the crucial time in which to socialise your puppy and expose him to as many 'things' as possible, for example, veterinarians, adults, children, dogs, cats, trucks, cars, skateboards, slippery floors.

Indy

Introduce sounds around the home such as the vacuum cleaner, hairdryer and washing machine.

Handle your puppy as much as possible and make everything a positive experience by rewarding him with lots of praise and treats.

Encourage other people from all walks of life to gently handle the puppy. This is a very important time to expose your puppy to enjoyable experiences with children. A negative experience at this age may affect your pup for his entire life so active supervision around children is the key.

Many vets and dog training schools offer puppy classes for puppies from 8 to 16 weeks of age where pups can safely interact with other puppies and also start learning

basic manners. Puppy classes are invaluable for pups to learn important life skills and are also an opportunity for you to ask questions and learn about training. It is a good idea to involve the whole family in puppy classes, so that everyone follows the same rules at home.

Dusty

Training can begin from the moment you bring your puppy home and you would be amazed at how much a puppy absorbs from 8 weeks of age. The more effort you put in during these first few months, the greater your reward when you have a reliable, friendly and obedient family pet.

PUPPY PLAYPEN

What you need

- A suitable playpen
- Bedding
- A bowl of water
- A toilet area, for example newspaper, wee pads or artificial turf
- Lots of chew toys such as Kong toys and raw bones

Why use a puppy playpen?

You can help your puppy learn good house etiquette if you use a playpen when he's unsupervised. Do not allow a puppy unsupervised time in the house before he has learned what he's allowed to chew and where to toilet.

Puppies and dogs who are permanently relegated to the backyard are more likely to engage in nuisance behaviours, such as barking, hyperactivity and destructive chewing. You will also be less likely to interact with your puppy when he is outside.

A puppy playpen will:

- Prevent mistakes.
- Make sure the puppy can't have toileting accidents in inappropriate places.
- Provide a safe place to leave your puppy for short or long periods of time, for example, while you're at work, sleeping, cooking dinner or watching TV.

- Remove the temptation of chewing inappropriate items and focus the puppy on chewing objects/toys you have provided as there are no other options.
- Help your puppy to settle into the house.
- Give you peace of mind and a little break!

Confinement should not mean isolation. A puppy playpen should be a suitable size for your puppy and set up in the main living area of the family home.

There are commercial puppy playpens available which are excellent and escape-proof.

In one corner, provide a bed, his food and water. In another corner, provide a toilet area. Unless you are actively playing with or supervising your puppy, he should be in his area.

HOUSE-TRAINING

What you need

- Lots of treats
- A puppy playpen
- Newspaper or wee pads for the playpen

Training guidelines

- The key to house-training your puppy is to set him up to win. Praise him and give him a food treat every time he eliminates in the desired area. Make a big fuss so that your pup understands he has done something that makes you very happy and also reward him.

Archie

- An 8-week-old puppy has a small bladder capacity, so you must offer frequent opportunities to go outside. Make sure you wait with him, so each time he eliminates you are there to reward him.
- Puppies always relieve themselves shortly after they wake up and also after a meal. You should immediately take your puppy outside after waking or eating, wait patiently until he goes, and then reward him with treats and praise. The whole process usually takes about 3 minutes.
- Puppies like to sniff the ground and turn circles before they eliminate. If you see this behaviour, be quick to whisk him outside before he has an accident. If you catch your puppy in the act, pick him up and take him swiftly outside and wait patiently to see if he finishes. Reward him with a treat and praise if he does.

Risk

Pearl

- **Do not let your pup roam free in the house.** If you are leaving your pup unattended for a period of time, then wake your pup up before you leave and take him outside to eliminate. You should then confine him to his playpen with something suitable to eliminate on, such as newspaper. If you can't actively supervise your pup when you are at home, then pop him in the playpen with something to chew. Read more about playpens on page 24.
- **Introduce a command** that works for you, like 'Wee-wees' or 'Go pee', and say this every time your pup eliminates. He will start associating these words with the action. This can be very handy, for

example, if you are travelling or visiting someone and want to be sure he has eliminated first.

- It's a good idea to immediately have a game or walk after your pup eliminates to make him understand that after he eliminates, he will be rewarded with a fun activity.
- If you are away from home with your pup (for example, in the park or having a walk), be sure to still offer praise and treats if he eliminates somewhere appropriate.
- If your pup has an accident, punishing him or rubbing his nose in it simply will not work. It will make your puppy scared of you or reluctant to eliminate in front of you.

CRATE TRAINING

What you need

- A crate suitable for the size of your puppy that is large enough for your puppy to be able to stand up and lie down stretched out
- Chew toys
- Bedding

What is crate training?

Crate training is the process of getting your puppy or dog to accept a crate as a safe location. Puppies quickly learn to love their crate as their own special place/den and will be comfortable in a crate whether at home, travelling, visiting friends or staying in a hotel.

Why use a crate?

- Using a dog crate to keep your pup confined short term really helps with housetraining.

- It provides your puppy with a safe bedroom of his own.
- It allows safe car travel for your puppy while also keeping your car safe from puppy teeth.
- Holidaying with your puppy will be easy. A lot of accommodation will allow puppies and dogs to stay if they are confined to a crate.
- Plane travel will be less stressful for your puppy or dog as airlines require that all puppies and dogs are confined to a crate

How to crate-train your puppy

- To start crate training, place special treats in the crate to encourage your puppy inside, also feed him his meals in there with the door left open.
- Once he is happy going in the crate, you can start closing the door for short periods. Be sure to reward him for calm, quiet behaviour.
- If your puppy whines or barks, be sure to wait for him to be quiet for a few seconds before rewarding him or letting him out.
- Gradually increase the time your puppy is left in his crate.
- As puppies rarely urinate or defecate near their sleeping area, they will hold on when confined and will usually eliminate as soon as you take them out.
- You need to give a young pup an opportunity to eliminate every hour and then give him lots of praise when he does.
- By not allowing your pup to make a mess inside, he quickly learns that he gets rewarded for going outside.
- This method makes housetraining easy but it does require you to be home with your pup during the day.

CHEWING

Breeze

Chewing is natural for puppies. They are inquisitive and will chew, dig and eat everything they can find. Shoes, hoses, brooms, mats, pot plants and garbage are all fair game. Chewing also helps relieve the pain associated with teething.

Chewing behaviour usually eases substantially by 12 months for most puppies but can become a lifelong habit if your puppy is not well managed.

A puppy playpen will solve most of your chewing issues. Puppies can be placed in their playpen whenever no-one is able to supervise their actions. This way the puppy doesn't get the chance to make mistakes. Provide plenty of chew toys and raw bones to keep him occupied. See pages 24–25 for setting up a playpen.

Provide suitable chew toys. Young dogs enjoy chewing and they need to chew while they are teething. Provide chew toys, changing them regularly to maintain your dog's interest.

Stuff a Kong toy with soaked dry food, wet food or chicken necks then place it in the freezer. This can be given to the puppy when he is left alone, together with some larger raw bones. Kongs make excellent chew toys and are almost indestructible. Don't give toys which can be easily torn apart or have squeakers in them that may be swallowed.

Puppy proof. Temporarily remove anything that your puppy might chew, such as plants, electrical cables and rugs. Until your puppy can be trusted not to chew your household items, he should not be given full run of the house unsupervised.

Do not leave your puppy unattended in the yard as there are far too many chewable temptations. Puppies love to do gardening but not necessarily to your standard!

Patience. If your puppy does chew up your favourite shoe or piece of furniture, remember you are the one who left him unsupervised. There is no point getting angry after the fact because your puppy will not know what he has done. Just clean up the mess without a fuss and make sure you don't leave him unsupervised again.

Pearl

PLAY-BITING OR MOUTHING

Play-biting is normal puppy behaviour. Although a puppy's jaws are not yet strong, a play-bite can really hurt as puppies have razor-sharp teeth. We need to teach pups to control their bite.

Play-biting does not mean your puppy will bite as an adult dog. Puppies will grow out of play-biting regardless of what we do. We certainly don't want to ruin our relationship by over-reacting to play-biting.

Risk

If one puppy bites another too hard when playing together, the other puppy will yelp and stop playing. Puppies learn to bite more softly to continue play. It is essential to let your puppy know when he has gone too far. A simple

'Ouch' is usually sufficient and stop playing with him. Give the puppy a minute or two of time-out before returning to play. Encourage the puppy to play-bite with a toy in exchange for your hand.

Have a plan of what you are going to do when your puppy play-bites. You can redirect his teeth onto an appropriate toy, give the puppy something else to do or ask the puppy for another task, such as to SIT, DROP or do a trick. Be sure to reward his compliance with food, or give him a time-out if he's too excited.

Puppies love movement and will often chase and bite your feet as you walk. If this happens, stop moving and when your puppy stops, give him a treat or a game with his favourite toy. This is a behaviour your puppy will grow out of very quickly if he doesn't get the opportunity to practise.

Avoid rough play with your puppy as this will encourage nipping behaviour. Young children should not be left unsupervised with puppies as they often excite them which, in turn, initiates nipping.

Cinch

JUMPING UP

It is natural for puppies (and dogs) to want to jump up when they are greeting people because it's fun and they are excited. This behaviour is often reinforced as people find cute puppies irresistible and shower them with attention when they jump up.

Risk

Remember, jumping up may be cute as a puppy but it can be an annoying habit as an adult and dangerous with larger dogs.

The best way to teach your pup not to jump up is to completely ignore the behaviour. So, when he jumps, turn away from your pup, keep your hands by your side and don't give him any attention until his four paws are firmly planted on the ground. When this happens, be sure to shower him with treats. You must reward him for not jumping up.

All members of the house must agree to do the same thing.

Meanwhile, work on your puppy's SIT and STAY routine (see pages 46 to 53) using lots of treats as rewards. Your puppy can't jump up if he is sitting. Teach him that it is when he is sitting that he gets his greetings and attention.

Practise with distractions, such as the doorbell, and offering high-value treats, such as cheese or cabanossi.

Bluey

Have a treat jar near the door and ask your visitors to ignore the jumping up until he sits and they can give a treat for good manners. In time your pup will learn that the doorbell means a treat in return for a SIT.

PREVENTING FOOD AGGRESSION

The possibility of a dog guarding his food by growling and/or biting worries many dog owners, and understandably so. It is natural for a dog to want to protect his food bowl if he feels there is a threat of having his food taken away.

We need to teach our puppies to enjoy having people near their food bowl, as this will set them up to be adult dogs who are comfortable having people around while eating.

Start by preparing your puppy's food as normal and then place his bowl on the ground. Step far enough away from the bowl so that the pup isn't bothered by your presence. Allow your pup to enjoy

Tilly

his food without any interruptions. When he finishes, call his name and toss a few smallish, very tasty treats into his bowl (suggestions include cooked chicken, cheese, sausage, cabanossi, sardines). Throw the treats into his bowl at the end of his meals as often as possible.

Always use a pleasant tone of voice when you call your pup's name and remember to stay far enough from the bowl so that he has no need to show any concern.

After a week or so of doing this, your pup should be comfortable with you standing close. You know he understands the game when he anticipates his treat is coming. This way the pup has a reason to enjoy you coming near his bowl.

An adult dog who anticipates a treat when someone approaches the food bowl will usually move back happily and show no reluctance to accept a person touching or moving the bowl.

Avoid feeding your pup outside in isolation – instead, always make sure there is activity going on around him while he is eating.

Do not allow your dog to be fed by a child without adult supervision, and always take special care when children are around .

Seek professional help if your puppy or adult dog is consistently guarding his bowl.

> **TIP**
>
> For many years, the common belief was that it was best to practise removing the food bowl from a pup while he was eating. We now encourage the opposite – we don't want pups to believe we steal from them as this may give them reason to guard their food. Instead, we keep adding to the bowl.

FEARS AND PHOBIAS

Some puppies bound through puppyhood and adolescence full of confidence and not fazed by anything. **It's also quite common for puppies to go through fear periods** at certain stages of their development, and if carefully managed, these puppies will grow out of it. However, it must be acknowledged that due to their genetic make-up, some puppies will always lack confidence.

When a puppy is startled or frightened he may display behaviours such as running and hiding, barking, crying or howling. It is important for you to recognise what has frightened him in order for you to be able to help him.

Many owners inadvertently encourage their dog to display fear by patting and verbally reassuring him when he is frightened. This reinforces that his fearful behaviour is OK.

Dusty

If you find your puppy in a stressful situation, then in a very calm and quiet manner try and move the puppy to a safe distance from whatever frightened or startled him. Most puppies need to observe from a comfortable distance and feel safe before gaining confidence to venture closer. We need to reward and encourage the confident

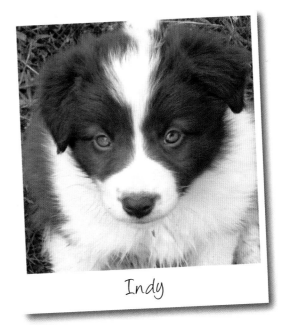

Indy

behaviour and try to ignore the frightened behaviour.

Never force your puppy to face his fears by placing him too close to whatever concerns him.

The best way to avoid problems is to socialise your puppy by exposing him to as many different situations as possible when young (see the chapter Socialisation, page 22).

There are some puppies and dogs that may need professional help for them to be able to live with their phobias. If you feel your puppy isn't progressing in overcoming his fears and phobias, then we would recommend you seek professional help as soon as possible.

PART 2
WONDERDOG TRAINING

TOP TRAINING TIPS

Set your dog up to win and always have fun

Flynn

You can start training your puppy from the minute you bring him home.

You absolutely can teach an older dog new tricks.

Keep training sessions short. A dog has a short attention span so keep training sessions to 5 minutes, two or three times a day.

Training must be a positive experience, so don't train your dog if you are in a bad mood or distracted. Losing your temper will only make your dog scared of you.

Buy yourself a 'bum bag' or treat pouch, as they free up both your hands and the treats are easily accessible for a quick reward.

When using food treats, you can use a proportion of your dog's everyday dry food if there are no distractions. However, if there are distractions or you are teaching something new, you will need high-value treats, such as tiny bits of chicken, cabanossi or cheese.

Consistency is the key – all members of the household must agree to the same rules and use the same key words and hand signals.

Make an effort to attend training classes as these not only help teach your dog basic obedience, but also social skills as well. In order to teach the tricks in this book, your dog must understand the basic commands of SIT, STAY, DROP and COME (THE RECALL).

Always let your dog know he has finished training with a release word such as OK and end on a happy note by playing a quick game or giving him his favourite toy.

Training should be fun – training provides mental stimulation for your dog and enhances the bond and trust between you.

SIT

SIT is a basic command that all dogs should know. It allows you to have easy control of your dog and makes it simple to groom, attach the lead, give tablets and examine her. If your dog sits when told, then you have the basics for good manners around people and food, as well as the prerequisite skill for tricks like **SIT PRETTY** and **SHAKE HANDS**.

WHAT YOU NEED

- A hungry dog – because she will be motivated by her treats
- A quiet room with no distractions
- Some treats

Willow

WONDERDOG STEPS

1 Attract your dog's attention with a food treat while she is standing.

2 Hold the treat above her nose and gently lift the treat upwards and backwards, keeping the food in direct contact with your dog's nose as she tilts her head backwards.

3 Most dogs will naturally move into the SIT position.

4 Say 'SIT' as soon as your dog starts moving into position. Immediately reward her with the treat and praise.

5 Repeat the command 'SIT' 10 to12 times a session and always before your dog's meal time.

6 Once your dog has mastered SIT, start practising with distractions and in different locations, always rewarding and showering your dog with praise as soon as she SITS. Just because your dog understands how to sit in one location doesn't mean she will understand to do this somewhere new.

7 If you find your dog jumping up for the food, don't get cross. Just ignore her behaviour and try again. Your dog will learn that when she doesn't get it right, she doesn't get a treat, but when she does, good things happen.

8 To continue the training, begin asking your dog to SIT before any action or event, such as before meals, before you put her lead on, and before you both walk out the door. Only when your dog SITS quietly do you proceed.

If there are no distractions, you can use a portion of your dog's everyday dry food as a treat. Your dog might as well be earning some of her food. However, if there are lots of distractions, like other dogs, children or noises, the reward needs to be high-value — for example, tiny bits of chicken, cheese or cabanossi.

TIP

STAY

STAY is a necessity for any Wonderdog, so that you have control of him at all times. This is an important command for safety reasons, so you can ask your dog not to move from a position and to be calm in public places or when you have visitors. In time your dog will learn that **STAY** means to hold whatever position he is in, whether it is **BEGGING**, **BOWING** or just lying on his bed.

WHAT YOU NEED
- A dog who can **SIT**
- A lead for when you're not in a confined area
- A confined area
- Treats

Flynn

WONDERDOG STEPS

1 Stand next to your dog.

2 Ask him to SIT and don't move away from him.

3 When he is still, say 'STAY' and reward him only while he is sitting still. You must not move either.

4 If your dog moves from the SIT position, gently place him back and start again.

5 Be patient and practise until your dog will SIT for a minute by your side.

6 Include a hand signal which is an open palm each time you say 'STAY'.

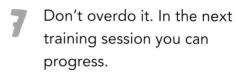

7 Don't overdo it. In the next training session you can progress.

8 Ask your dog to SIT next to you and take a step back as you give the command to STAY. If he sits on his mark, then you can immediately reward him with a treat. If he breaks the SIT just move him back to the exact starting point each time. He'll soon learn that to earn the treat he needs to stay still.

9 Gradually increase your distance until you are confident that your dog has understood your request.

10 If you are not in a safe confined area you will need a lead for safety.

11 Gradually add distractions and reward your dog with praise and treats when he doesn't move.

12 Your dog needs to grasp the concept that moving is the wrong thing to do and that you are really happy when he stays still.

13 Once mastered in one location you can practise the command in other confined areas of the house and garden, and in other positions such as DROP.

14 Remember that your dog has a short attention span. There are many new things to see and places to explore, so practise the STAY for short periods of time only.

> This command needs lots of practice to be perfected. Think baby steps and take it slowly. Dogs get distracted, especially at the park where there are birds, other dogs to play with and people to meet. Make sure you perfect the 'STAY' at home before attempting it in a new location.

TIP

DROP/DOWN

The **DROP** is an important command for the safety of your dog as it enables you to have control in all situations — for example, at home, in the park and at the vet clinic. It is also a prerequisite to learning **ROLL OVER** or **BANG**

WHAT YOU NEED
- A dog who can **SIT**
- Treats

Jinx

WONDERDOG STEPS

1 Ask your dog to SIT and reward her with a treat.

2 Hold a treat in front of your dog's nose and slowly move the treat towards the ground. As she reaches for the treat, place it on the ground and slide it along the ground in an L-shaped movement.

3 You must keep contact between the treat and your dog's nose, and her body should naturally follow.

4 Use the command DROP and as soon as she is down, reward her with the treat.

5 Practise several times. The DROP isn't quite as easy as the SIT and it will require some patience. If the dog's bottom comes up, repeat the above steps but move your hand more slowly to the ground.

6 Start including a hand signal of a downward stroke each time you say 'DROP'.

7 Once your dog has mastered DROP from the SIT position, you can start teaching her from the stand position, or even from walking. The hand signal will be clear to your dog, even from a distance.

When you are training your dog, at the end of each command, be sure to give a release word such as 'OK' so that your dog knows when she is free to move.

TIP

THE RECALL

This is an important command for your dog's safety, as it teaches her to come to you whenever you call, no matter where you are. It is much easier to teach this command to a puppy than an adult dog. Please take your time with these lessons. If you get the **RECALL** right from puppyhood, your entire experience as a dog owner is going to be more pleasurable.

WHAT YOU NEED
- A squeaky toy
- A long lead
- Some treats

Jordie

WONDERDOG STEPS

1. The key to this command is teaching your dog that coming to you is a pleasant experience. Of course she will want to come to you if she gets her favourite toy, some food and verbal praise from you when she does.

2. Start calling 'COME' around meals and play times, always telling her what a good girl she is, even though she was going to come anyway. You are programming her action to the word COME.

3 Practise moving backwards and squeaking a toy, so your dog follows. Always include the command COME as you move.

4 Over time you will have programmed your dog to run towards you each time she hears the word COME. Encourage her with a squeaky toy, treats and verbal praise.

5 Don't keep calling your dog when she's not coming. You may now be teaching your dog to run away when she hears you call 'COME'.

6 Your dog's safety is very important so if you are not in an enclosed area be sure to practise the RECALL on a long lead before considering letting your dog run free.

7 Progress to adding in distractions and different locations.

8 Puppies get easily distracted so keep their attention by offering high-value treats.

9 Start to include a hand signal of open arms with each repetition of the command.

10 Always give plenty of praise, make a fuss, and let her have her toy or treat when she does come to you. You have to make yourself more exciting than the other dogs, trees and people in the park or why would your dog bother returning at all?

Never punish or scream at your dog if she doesn't come back. That will only teach your dog to be reluctant to come back next time.

TIP

PART 3

WONDERDOG
TRICKS

WHY TEACH TRICKS?

Dogs are very intelligent and need to have their minds occupied to prevent boredom. Tricks provide physical and mental stimulation for your dog, as well as improving your relationship with him and developing trust. Remember, dogs are also very social animals that enjoy spending time with us, and training is a wonderful way to spend quality time together. This includes puppies as well as adult dogs. The first 10 tricks (**SHAKE HANDS** to **FETCH**) can be taught to puppies as well as adult dogs.

Teaching your dog tricks is fun and rewarding for you both. It's entertaining and gives you the chance to show friends just how clever your canine friend is.

SHAKE HANDS

This trick teaches your dog to make human friends quickly by shaking hands to say 'hello'. For more fun, you can teach your dog to shake her right or left paw on request.

WHAT YOU NEED
- A dog who **SITS**
- Treats

Willow

WONDERDOG STEPS

1 Ask your dog to SIT.

2 Get down to her level and kneel before her. Reward her with a treat for sitting.

3 Hold out your left hand, palm up, and reach for your dog's right paw (that is the paw directly in front of you), reassuring her as you gently pick up the paw (scratching behind the paw helps).

4 Encourage your dog by telling her 'YES' and then command 'SHAKE' as you softly shake her paw.

5 Reward your dog with a treat, even though it is you who is doing all the work at this point. You are really rewarding her for her cooperation while teaching her you want to hold her paw.

6 Once she is used to you saying 'SHAKE' and lifting her paw, try hesitating and she will probably offer her paw to you as she knows that she'll get a treat. Catch her paw as soon as she starts to lift it and help her out, always saying 'SHAKE' and always rewarding her.

7 Don't forget to give her the release word OK when you have finished and put her paw back down.

8 Once mastered you can say 'SHAKE RIGHT' when you lift the right paw.

9 Commence the whole process again with your right hand reaching for her left paw and saying 'SHAKE LEFT'. Help her as necessary until she realises she now has to lift the other paw. Repeat and reward as before.

10 Do the left and right paws separately during each training session and don't try to do them together until your dog clearly understands what you are asking. Your dog should learn to extend whichever paw your arm is reaching towards.

This is a great first trick for puppies and you can start teaching it as soon as you have taught your puppy to SIT.

TIP

GIVE ME FIVE AND TEN

This trick is very cute and a fun progression from **SHAKE HANDS**.
You are teaching your dog to lift his paw in response to you
holding your palm up to him.

WHAT YOU NEED
- A dog who can **SHAKE HANDS**
- Treats

Flynn

WONDERDOG STEPS

1 Ask your dog to SIT. Then kneel before him and offer your hand towards the leg directly in front of you.

2 Ask your dog to SHAKE HANDS. Instead of shaking his paw, lay it flat on your palm and say 'GIVE ME FIVE'. Reward him with a treat.

3 Practise until your dog is offering his paw to you when you offer him your palm near the ground.

4 Gradually turn your hand so it is facing your dog and start moving it up towards shoulder level. Your aim is to get your dog to reach up and tap your palm.

5 Practise with both right and left paws, using the GIVE ME FIVE command.

6 Once perfected with each paw, offer both hands and say 'GIVE ME TEN'. Some dogs will automatically try to give you both paws. Shower your dog with praise and encouragement.

7 If he offers only one paw, withhold the treat and try again.

8 If you have perfected each paw, most dogs will take your cue when you offer two hands.

For larger dogs like Flynn, you may need to lower your hands for the GIVE ME TEN until they develop more balance.

TIP

TAKE A BOW

All good performers know how to acknowledge their audience. The Wonderdogs take a bow at the end of their stage performances as a way of saying goodbye to their fans. Willow likes to acknowledge her audiences when finishing on stage and she always ends with a **BOW**. This is another trick Willow mastered as a puppy.

WHAT YOU NEED
• Treats

Willow

WONDERDOG STEPS

1 Lure your dog to stand.

2 Kneel down to your dog's level and support her hindquarters with your arm.

3 With a food treat, encourage her head towards the ground while keeping her hindquarters elevated.

4 Reward her with the treat even if she bends down just a little.

5 Repeat the command 'TAKE A BOW' each time your dog leans forward.

6 Many dogs will try to lie down. Persevere with the hindquarter support and use the treat for motivation.

7 As soon as you feel your dog understands the movement, ask her to STAY and she should hold the position. Don't remove your supporting arm until you are confident she will stay in the BOW position.

8 Always reward her and don't forget the release word OK so she knows when to stop.

9 If she stands up before you ask her to, reposition her and start again.

10 Include a hand signal, such as pointing your hand towards the ground, when you say 'TAKE A BOW'.

Bowing is a natural behaviour for dogs. They 'play bow' when they meet other dogs that they want to play with. If you see your dog doing the BOW, you are halfway there and can really use this to your advantage. Praise and reward this behaviour and include the word 'BOW' whenever she does this pose.

TIP

ROLL OVER

This is a fantastic trick for puppies to learn. It's simple to teach and a lot of fun. Flynn had it mastered by 8 weeks of age!

WHAT YOU NEED
- A dog who **DROPS** and **STAYS**
- Treats

Flynn

WONDERDOG STEPS

1 Begin with your dog in the DROP position and reward him with a treat.

2 Hold a treat in front of your dog's nose and slowly move your hand towards his shoulder. Your dog's nose should follow your direction until he rolls on his side. Reward him with the treat.

3 Repeat the above step until your dog finds it easy to lie on his side. Reward him for being on his side.

4 This time, with a treat in front of your dog's nose, slowly move your hand towards his shoulder, then continue to move your hand over his back until he is lying on his back with his legs in the air. At this stage he will probably automatically roll onto his other side. Introduce the ROLL OVER command and then reward him with a treat and verbal praise.

5 Keep practising this trick until your dog will ROLL OVER when he hears you say 'ROLL OVER'.

6 Start including hand signals too.

7 Once your dog has perfected the ROLL OVER on one side, try teaching him to roll the other way.

8 The final step is for you to be able to stand up while asking him to ROLL OVER. Be sure to reward him with verbal praise and a treat.

There are several movements involved in this trick. You will need a few sessions with your dog until he learns to ROLL OVER from the DROP position. Ensure you have plenty of treats on hand to help him along.

TIP

SPIN

This trick is great because there is lots of action and movement, and dogs tend to get really excited about having an excuse to jump around and be silly.

WHAT YOU NEED
• Tasty treats

WONDERDOG STEPS

1 Lure your dog to stand.

2 Get her attention focused on the treat you are holding in your hand.

Jordie

3 With your dog's nose following the treat, start moving your hand in an arc so that her head and body follow your movement.

4 Tell her to SPIN and reward her with the treat when she starts moving in a circle. Try to encourage her to put her head as close as possible to her body as she turns.

5 Start slowly, moving your hand to form a large circle, and gradually make it smaller and quicker.

6 Start replacing the treat with a hand movement only and reward your dog once she is twirling.

CROSS PAWS

In this cute trick you are teaching your dog to 'behave like a lady' and cross one paw over the other while lying down.

WHAT YOU NEED

• A dog who can **SHAKE HANDS** or **GIVE ME FIVE OR TEN**

Jinx, Flynn and Willow

WONDERDOG STEPS

1 Ask your dog to DROP, then kneel before her and offer your hand low to the ground towards the leg directly in front of you.

2 Your dog should give you her paw. Keep reassuring and rewarding her with a food treat and verbal praise.

3 Practise until your dog offers her paw to you when you offer her your palm near the ground.

4 Gradually move your hand across towards her other leg. Ask her to CROSS PAWS and reward her with a treat. The aim is to get your dog to lift her paw over her other leg and place it down in a crossed position.

5 Once perfected, with your dog touching your hand with her paw, start moving your hand just out of reach and see what your dog does. Be sure to shower her with praise and encouragement at any attempt to cross her paws.

6 Your aim now is to be able to move away from your dog and for her to respond to your command.

7 Keep practising over several sessions if necessary until your dog attempts to cross her paws when you say 'CROSS PAWS'.

> Think of this trick as teaching your dog to shake paws from a DROP position. The key is to get her to extend her paw to you on an angle, crossing over the other leg.

TIP

HEAD DOWN/ SAD FACE

This is a great trick for whenever you want to pretend your dog is sad about something. The Wonderdogs love doing this trick as they get such a good response from people. We use this trick a lot when filming.

WHAT YOU NEED
- A dog who will **DROP**
- A dog who will **STAY**
- Treats

Jinx, Flynn and Willow

Jinx

WONDERDOG STEPS

1 Begin with your dog in the DROP position.

2 Let her see a treat in your hand but don't let her grab it. Lure her to move her head towards the ground using the treat as motivation while saying 'HEAD DOWN'.

3 Reward her with the treat if her head goes down, even if only for a second.

4 Keep practising over several sessions, rewarding her each time her head goes down.

5 Now start asking her to STAY when she puts her head down. If she holds the position, immediately give her the release word OK and reward her with a treat.

6 You may find your dog starting to put her head down naturally. Be sure to quickly reward her if she does.

7 Practise by asking her to STAY for longer periods of time and from further away.

8 If she does put her head up, don't give her the reward, and just start the process again.

9 Start including hand signals when you give the HEAD DOWN command.

10 Your aim is to be able to use either a hand signal or a verbal signal only for her to perform the HEAD DOWN trick.

> **Dogs will naturally place their head on the ground when they are tired. If you are quick to reward this position, she is likely to offer this behaviour again. Repetition is important.**

TIP

SIT PRETTY

This trick is always a party pleaser. Your dog sits up on her haunches and holds the position. She can then beg for food or her favourite toy.

WHAT YOU NEED
- A dog who can **SIT** and **STAY**, and do **GIVE ME TEN**
- Treats

Jordie and Jinx

Jordie

WONDERDOG STEPS

There are two ways to teach this trick.

First method

1 If your dog knows GIVE ME TEN, ask her to GIVE ME TEN and then reward her with a treat. Then ask for GIVE ME TEN again but this time hold your hands just out of reach. Reward her as soon as your dog is in the SIT PRETTY position.

2 Once your dog has found her balance for sitting on her haunches tell her to STAY and reward her as she holds the

position, even if she only manages it for a second at first. Always help her to balance if necessary.

3 Gradually increase the time she holds the position and say 'SIT PRETTY'.

4 Always remember to give your dog the release word OK when she is finished.

5 Keep practising over several sessions.

6 Once your dog has mastered SIT PRETTY and can hold the position, you can start to increase your distance from her when you give the command.

Second method

1 Begin with your dog sitting in front of you.

2 Hold a treat to your dog's nose and move your hand upwards to encourage her to lift her front paws off the ground.

3 As she lifts her front paws off the ground, say 'SIT PRETTY' and reward her with her treat and verbal praise.

4 The main problem with this method is that many dogs get excited and jump up for the treat or snatch it. Just ignore this behaviour and start again.

5 Repeat these steps several times, each time asking your dog to lift her paws a little higher to enable her to find her balance.

Some dogs might need a little help to find their balance on their haunches, especially bigger dogs.

TIP

LEG WEAVE

This trick is very impressive and a lot of fun.
You are teaching your dog to weave
in and out of your legs
as you walk.

WHAT YOU NEED
• Lots of food treats
• Good balance!

Willow

WONDERDOG STEPS

1 Call your dog to your left side and reward her.

2 Hold a treat in your right hand and move your right leg forward. Now you have a gap for your dog to walk through.

3 While in this position, show your dog the treat in your right hand by putting your hand under your right leg. Reward her as she moves towards your hand and lure her through your legs.

4 Practise this until your dog is following the food lure easily. Be sure to reward her each time she walks through your legs.

5 Once perfected on the left side, repeat the whole process on the right side.

6 As your dog is moving under your leg be sure to say 'WEAVE' and keep rewarding her with treats and praise

7 Once she can WEAVE on command from both sides, it's time to see if she can WEAVE when you are walking very slowly.

8 You may need to keep encouraging her for a while and be in a slightly crouched position until she understands the command.

9 Your aim now is to get your dog to WEAVE on command without luring her at each step and for you to be able to stand upright.

10 Keep practising over several sessions but be very careful not to stand on your dog's paw, which may cause her to lose confidence.

Take your time to perfect this trick, encouraging your dog at each stage. This trick is a team effort and Willow encourages you to see how fast you can walk with your dog weaving between your legs.

TIP

FETCH

A true Wonderdog must be able to retrieve different objects with his mouth, before he can master all the required tricks. Flynn likes to be helpful at home and will carry bags, slippers and flowers. He's a real ladies' man.

WHAT YOU NEED

- A soft toy to start (dogs prefer to hold something soft)
- A confined area
- An excited dog

Flynn

WONDERDOG STEPS

1 In a confined area such as your backyard or inside your house, attract your dog's attention to a soft toy by moving it around and teasing him with it.

2 When he wants to play with it, gently roll it along the ground, so that he wants to chase it. Don't throw it far.

3 Encourage him to pick up the toy, telling him excitedly to FETCH.

4 When he has the toy in his mouth, gently call him to COME and reward him with a treat or another favourite toy.

5 You need to teach him to keep the toy in his mouth and bring it back to you. If you step towards him, he will probably drop the toy but if you move away from him, he is more likely to come to you.

6 As he does step towards you, encourage him verbally in an excited tone.

7 If he drops the toy, make a game out of it and quickly send him to FETCH it again.

8 Praise him for bringing the toy towards you but don't take the toy off him too quickly as he may be reluctant to bring it back to you next time.

9 Practise these steps, encouraging your dog to chase the toy, FETCH it and bring it back to you in exchange for another toy or treat.

10 Once this trick is mastered you can move on to teaching him to fetch different items.

> **Sometimes dogs love holding their toys so much that they don't want to let go. This can usually be solved by offering a tasty treat while you gently take hold of the toy with your other hand. The treat will nearly always win over the toy.**

TIP

FIND IT

This trick is a great way to impress your friends when you are leaving the house and also very useful if you often misplace your keys. It involves teaching your dog to use her acute sense of smell.

WHAT YOU NEED

- A dog that **FETCHES**
- Strong-smelling treats (it is best to begin with treats and progress to objects like keys)
- Her favourite toy
- A towel or newspaper

Jordie

WONDERDOG STEPS

1 Call your dog and show her your treat. Ask her to STAY and keep her attention while you place the treat under the towel or spread-out newspaper. Don't make it too difficult the first time, as she may lose interest.

2 Release your dog with 'OK' and tell her to FIND IT, encouraging her to help herself to the treat. Make a fuss, and praise her for finding the treat.

3 If she has trouble finding the treat, help her out by not covering it completely for the first few attempts.

4 Start covering the treat completely with the towel or newspaper, making it more difficult to find. Encourage her with urgency in your voice, so she finds it as quickly as possible and doesn't get bored.

5 Start hiding the treat in different locations, but near the starting point, so your dog has to sniff it out.

6 Once your dog has mastered finding treats, then you can move to objects like her favourite toy or your keys. Use the same principle as with the treats. Allow her to sniff the object in your hand and then ask her to FIND IT after you have hidden it somewhere easy for her.

7 Reward her with a treat when she returns the object to you.

8 Gradually increase the difficulty of the hiding place as you did with the treat.

> It's possible to teach dogs to retrieve a large number of objects. Jordie often uses this trick around the house. She enjoys the challenge of finding different things and often gets the job of finding the keys or mobile phone when they are missing.

TIP

HIDE FACE

Flynn loves this trick as people always laugh at him when he's asked 'Have you been bad today?' and he hides his face by putting his paw over his nose.

WHAT YOU NEED
- A dog who can **DROP** and **STAY**
- Sticky paper notes
- Treats

Flynn and Willow

Flynn

WONDERDOG STEPS

1 Kneel before your dog and ask him to DROP.

2 Very gently place a sticky paper note on your dog's nose, reassuring him as you do so. You will need to be quick as most dogs will lift their paw up to wipe their face as soon as you put the sticky note on.

3 When your dog wipes his face, say 'HIDE FACE' and be sure to reward him.

4 Keep practising with the sticky notes, repeating 'HIDE FACE' each time he wipes his face.

5 Gradually reduce the size of the sticky note. Continue to give the command HIDE FACE each time you place the note on his nose.

6 Once your dog has perfected this trick with the sticky paper notes, you will need to see what he does when you excitedly say 'HIDE FACE' without the sticky note on his face. Some dogs will automatically lift their paw to wipe their face. Shower your dog with praise and encouragement at any attempt to lift his paw off the ground and towards his face.

7 Over time you can ask your dog to STAY while his paw is hiding his face.

8 To make this trick a little harder you could try HIDE FACE while your dog is sitting.

> The success of this trick depends on your dog understanding that STAY means holding whatever position you are asking him to. So, be confident that your dog understands this concept before commencing this trick.

TIP

TOUCH FOOT

This shows that your dog is ambidextrous. What really impresses people is when your dog knows her right from her left paw. If you are really clever you may be able to use only a foot cue to get her to do this trick.

WHAT YOU NEED

- Treats
- A dog who can **SHAKE HANDS**
- Good balance

Jordie

WONDERDOG STEPS

1 Ask your dog to SIT.

2 Reach down to her level.

3 Hold out your left hand, palm up, and ask for her right paw. Reassure her as you go and be sure to reward her with a treat when she gives you her right paw.

4 Encourage your dog by saying 'YES' and then ask her to SHAKE each time she touches your palm.

5 Slowly move your left hand closer to your left foot and ask for her paw. Repeat this step and then reward her.

6 Now hold out your left foot and your left hand and then ask for her right paw. Try to remove your hand and leave just your foot for her paw to touch. Keep rewarding her each time she uses her paw.

7 Try holding out your foot and asking for her paw and she will probably offer her paw to you as she knows that is how she gets her treats. Catch her paw with your foot as soon as she starts to lift it and help her out, always saying 'TOUCH FEET' and always rewarding her.

8 Don't forget to give her the release word OK when you have finished and put her paw back down.

9 Then commence the whole process again with your right hand. Hold out your right foot and your right hand then ask for her left paw. Try to remove your hand and leave just your foot for her paw to touch. Keep rewarding her each time she touches your foot with her paw.

10 Repeat and reward as before.

Teach her the left and right paws separately. Your dog should learn to extend whichever paw mirrors your extended foot.

TIP

JUMP THROUGH ARMS

This trick showcases your dog's athletic ability. Once perfected, there are no props required and applause is guaranteed!

WHAT YOU NEED
- A dog who will **SIT** and **STAY**
- A Hula-Hoop
- A favourite toy
- A corridor

Willow

WONDERDOG STEPS

1 Hold the hoop at a right angle to the wall of the corridor. The bottom of the hoop should be touching the floor. We use the wall as a barrier so your dog has no choice but to go in the direction you are asking.

2 Ask your dog to SIT and STAY on one side of the hoop.

3 Get her attention as you put her favourite toy or a treat on the other side of the hoop.

4 Encourage her to go through the hoop to get the toy or treat. She probably won't even notice the hoop until you slowly start lifting it off the ground, making her jump a little.

5 As she lifts her feet to jump say the command 'THROUGH' and then 'YES' when she makes it through to retrieve her toy or treat.

6 Repeat the above steps, always commencing with your dog in the SIT position. Only raise the hoop a centimetre at a time and only when you are confident your dog is competent at each height.

7 Once the hoop is a certain height, your dog may choose to go under rather than through it. If she does, ignore her and return to the starting point.

8 Practise in the corridor, so she is always confined by the wall, before attempting the trick in an open space. When you do venture somewhere else, start at a low level again and use lots of praise and rewards.

9 Now you can teach your dog to jump through your arms. Basically you just follow the above steps, replacing the hoop with your arms held out to form a circle.

> **For puppies, this trick must be performed low to the ground so they don't damage their growing joints. Some dogs may be too big to jump through your arms, so for their safety, stick to hoops.**

TIP

BANG

This is where you point your fingers like a gun at your dog and say **'BANG'**. Your dog falls to the ground and plays dead.

This trick is a modified fun version of **ROLL OVER**, but far more impressive because you progress to teach your dog to do it from the **SIT** position so there is a lot of movement. This is one of Flynn's favourite positions, he even likes to sleep like this. He also knows that small children like to pat him on his chest while he's in this position.

WHAT YOU NEED
- A dog who knows how to **SIT**, **DROP** and **STAY**
- Treats

Jordie and Flynn

WONDERDOG STEPS

1 Begin with your dog in the DROP position and reward him with a treat.

2 Hold a treat in front of your dog's nose. Slowly move your hand towards his shoulder with his nose following and reward him with the treat. Repeat and eventually your dog will find it easy to lie on his side. Reward him for being on his side.

Flynn

3 Now hold a treat in front of your dog's nose, and slowly move your hand towards his shoulder, then continue to move your hand over his back until he is lying on his back with his legs in the air. You may need to help support him in this position to start with. Say 'BANG' and then reward him with the treat.

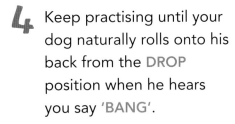

4 Keep practising until your dog naturally rolls onto his back from the DROP position when he hears you say 'BANG'.

5 Start including a hand signal of fingers pointing like a gun.

6 Once perfected from the DROP position, commence from the SIT position. Go slowly as he needs to SIT then DROP then ROLL OVER.

7 The final step is asking him to hold the position when he is on his back with his legs in the air. This is just a matter of asking him to STAY when in this position. Be sure to reassure him with verbal praise.

8 Always release your dog from being 'dead' with an 'OK'.

9 Once your dog has mastered the trick, you can progress to teaching him to respond from a standing position, always using the same hand signal and verbal cue.

The key here is to take your time and not expect your dog to put it all together at once. Do several sessions just learning to ROLL OVER before you consider progressing. Even the smartest dog can get confused when asked to do several movements at once.

TIP

SPEAK AND COUNT

Teaching your dog to **SPEAK** (bark on command) can be very impressive. You can ask your dog questions and amaze your friends when she barks the answer. Teaching your dog to speak also has the advantage of allowing you to teach your dog to be silent on request.

WHAT YOU NEED
- A favourite toy
- Treats

Left to right:

Flynn, Jinx, Willow, and Jordie

WONDERDOG STEPS

1 You must first figure out what it is that triggers your dog to bark. Perhaps it is excitement at seeing her favourite toy or maybe it is when there is someone at the door. You need to be able to anticipate her barking.

Jinx

2 Set your dog up in a situation where you know she will bark. As she does, excitedly say 'SPEAK' followed by 'GOOD GIRL' and reward her with a treat (or her toy if that's what made her bark).

3 Repeat the above steps a few times. Most dogs enjoy being rewarded for barking and pick this up quite quickly.

4 Start incorporating a hand signal with your verbal command and keep on practising.

5 Next, say 'QUIET' and give a 'Shhh!' hand signal. Reward your dog with a treat or toy as soon as she stops barking. You want her to learn that she barks only until you stop your signal.

6 You can help your dog learn to be QUIET by holding a treat near her nose, as she will stop barking to sniff it. Make sure you tell her 'QUIET', followed by 'GOOD GIRL' and then give her the reward when she is quiet.

7 Practise while you are nearby and then gradually start moving further away from your dog. Always make sure you have your dog's full attention so that she is watching your hand signals.

8 Now you can teach your dog to count. Firstly, ask for one bark before saying 'QUIET'.

9 Practise doing one bark only until you are sure she understands that one hand signal means one bark.

10 As you give the hand signal, also nod your head once and don't forget to reward her with a treat and praise.

11 Once your dog knows one hand signal and one nod equals one bark, try doing two hand signals with two head nods. Basically, you are asking her to SPEAK, SPEAK but without the words.

12 Progress to SPEAK, SPEAK, SPEAK, that is, three hand signals and three head nods.

13 Practise counting from one to three, gradually removing the hand signals and using nods only. With time, you can reduce that nod to the slightest movement or even a blink.

14 As soon as your dog hits the target number, applaud her by clapping or saying excitedly 'CLEVER GIRL'. You are cutting her off before she can keep barking. Once she knows to bark when you nod, getting her to count to ten is no more difficult for her than counting to two.

> Jinx sometimes gets a little carried away and loves the sound of her voice. We are very careful to let her know that being QUIET is just as important as SPEAKING. Sometimes she'll bark for attention, and we never reward her for this.
>
> **TIP**

PUT TOYS AWAY

A great trick to show that your dog is not only smart but neat and tidy too. Grandma Willow needs to teach this trick to messy Flynn, who just loves to play with all the toys and leaves them lying around.

WHAT YOU NEED
- A dog who will **CARRY** objects, **FETCH** and **RELEASE** them on command
- A basket or box
- A soft toy
- Treats

Willow

WONDERDOG STEPS

1 Commence with a soft toy and a basket or box that is fairly low to the ground.

2 Ask your dog to FETCH the object as usual. When your dog returns, make sure you are standing next to the basket. Reward her with a treat.

3 Ask her to GIVE or RELEASE the object. As she releases the object grab it and drop it in the basket. Say 'BASKET' at the same time.

4 Repeat this several times until your dog releases the object when she gets to the basket. You can help out as necessary by directing the object into the basket.

5 Eventually, you want to move the basket away from you and be able to ask your dog to retrieve the toy and place it in the basket unaided.

6 The key word is BASKET. Your dog must learn this doesn't just mean to retrieve the toy, but that she must follow through and place it in the basket.

7 As always, put lots of enthusiasm into your voice to get your dog excited about the task.

> Once you have mastered this trick, you can get your dog to tidy up all kinds of things. She can learn to place objects such as rubbish in the bin or to tidy her own toys away in a basket.

TIP

SPELL

This is a really popular trick that is a favourite with kids. It works by getting your dog to identify letters that have your scent on them.

WHAT YOU NEED

- Some large wooden letters from a handicraft shop. You need the letters you would like your dog to spell, plus a few extras
- A dog who knows how to **FETCH** and **HOLD** objects
- A pair of tongs

Flynn, Jinx and Willow

Jordie

WONDERDOG STEPS

1 Decide what word you want your dog to spell — for example, DOG.

2 Take only the letters D, O and G from the alphabet and handle them so that they are covered in your scent. Use the tongs to move the other letters so they do not have your scent on them.

3 Ask your dog to FETCH the letters D, O, G one at a time (it is unreasonable to expect her to get them in the right order). Practise several times just with these letters.

4 Once your dog is bringing D, O, G back to you, add other letters a couple at a time.

5 If she brings back D, O or G, shower her with praise. For any other letter, simply say nothing and send her again. Repeat until she brings back one of the desired letters.

6 Praise her when she does.

7 Your dog will soon learn that any letter with your scent on it is desirable and she will sniff those out and bring them to you.

> It is best to stick to words of three or four letters like DOG, CAT or FOOD. This keeps the momentum going and prevents the audience from getting bored.

TIP

DANCE

It's a real party pleaser when your dog has her own dance move.

WHAT YOU NEED

- Patience — depending on the dog, it may take a while for her to get used to balancing on her hind legs
- Treats

Jinx

WONDERDOG STEPS

1 Before you try this trick, consider your dog's breed, size and age to see if she is suitable. Large breeds, dogs with injuries and puppies under 12 months should avoid standing up on their hind legs.

2 Small dogs find it much easier to balance on their hind legs and won't need as much assistance as larger dogs. For a small dog, crouch down to her level and hold the treat above her head, so she has to reach for it. Many small

breeds will stand on their hind legs naturally, so we can reward this.

3 Encourage your dog to reach for the treat without allowing her to snatch it. Say 'DANCE' whenever she gets onto her back legs, but only give her the treat when she holds for a second or more. You can offer your arm for balance if necessary.

4 For medium to large dogs, hold your hands out just above your dog's head for her to touch.

5 You must allow your dog time to figure out her balance with your support. Do this over several short sessions and you can encourage her to move a couple of steps forwards and backwards with your help. The more practice she has, the more she will build up the strength she needs in her leg muscles to perform. Don't forget to reward her.

6 Start removing your assistance and encourage your dog to start balancing by herself. While balancing, say 'DANCE' and reward her with food and remember to praise her profusely if she holds the position for even a second.

Not all dogs can do this trick. As Wonderdog Willow got older she retired from this trick for safety. Jordie and Jinx on the other hand are perfectly built to DANCE and they love it.

TIP

TARGET STICK

This is something different and fun to teach. The aim is to teach your dog to **TOUCH** a target with his nose. Once your dog has mastered following and touching the **TARGET STICK** with his nose, you can gradually make it harder by moving the target stick and asking him to follow it, always touching with his nose. In time you can send your dog to touch the target no matter where he is.

Seal trainers use a target stick for lots of their tricks. You now have another tool to use in your training. For example, teaching your dog to **DANCE**, **SPIN** and many more tricks, by getting him to follow the **TARGET STICK**.

WHAT YOU NEED

- A **TARGET STICK.** This can be a piece of wooden dowel with a rubber ball or ping-pong ball stuck on the end, or even a kid's fairy wand
- Treats

Flynn

WONDERDOG STEPS

1 Dogs and puppies are very inquisitive, so when something new is shown to them they will go to investigate.

2 Start in a quiet location with no distractions.

3 Rub the end of the TARGET STICK with food to encourage your dog to investigate the smell.

4 Start with the TARGET STICK out of sight, then quickly show it to your dog. If he looks at it or goes near it say 'YES' and reward him with a treat, then hide the TARGET STICK behind your back again.

5 Repeat this many times.

6 Once your dog looks at the TARGET STICK, withhold the treat and see if he will touch it with his nose. When he does, say 'TOUCH' and reward him.

7 Now you won't need to rub food on the end any more.

8 Practise until your dog is consistently touching the TARGET STICK with his nose. Only then should you start moving the stick for him to follow over a short distance. Always reward him each time he touches it with his nose.

TIP

If you have a cat like Tigger who is motivated by food, targeting is easy to teach. Train your cat when he is hungry and you'll be surprised how easily he will pick this up. Young cats love using their paws to tap things, so you can have some fun and teach them to tap the target with their paw instead of their nose. Tigger often uses this trick in film and television work.

IN THE STUDIO

We spent two very long days in the studio to capture the photos for this book. We needed a balance of fun and serious shots and the Wonderdogs never let us down. These guys REALLY love to show off for the camera and are happiest when all the attention is on them. They never failed to hit their marks, perform their tricks and keep the show going, despite several attempts from Tigger the cat to pull the focus.

Thank you Willow, Jordie, Jinx and Flynn (and Tigger) for a job well done.

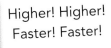

Jordie bangs out
some tunes
between shots.

Best friends
forever.

SHOWING OFF

Wonderdogs need to stay fit and they just love ball games.

They have to look after their film-star smiles.

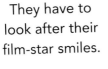

'We didn't do it!'

SCHOOL'S IN

The lesson today is understanding humans and how they think.

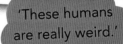

'These humans are really weird.'

TIGGER PLOTS A TAKEOVER

JUST HAVING FUN

While in the studio we let the dogs have plenty of play time between takes.

This is important for them and it gives us lots of laughs as their toys go flying through the air.

THANK YOU

Thank you to the following Wonderpuppies who contributed their best mischief to the making of the puppy section in this book.

Archie

Cinch

Dusty

Pearl

Clair

Zing

Indy

Risk

Breeze

Dougal

Bluey

Tilly

HarperCollins*Publishers*

First published in Australia in 2012
by HarperCollins*Publishers* Australia Pty Limited
ABN 36 009 913 517
harpercollins.com.au

Copyright © Dr Katrina Warren and Kelly Gill 2012

The rights of Dr Katrina Warren and Kelly Gill to be identified
as the authors of this work have been asserted by them under
the *Copyright Amendment (Moral Rights Act) 2000*.

This work is copyright. Apart from any use as permitted under the
Copyright Act 1968, no part may be reproduced, copied, scanned,
stored in a retrieval system, recorded, or transmitted, in any form
or by any means, without the prior written permission of the publisher.

HarperCollins*Publishers*
Level 13, 201 Elizabeth Street, Sydney NSW 2000, Australia
31 View Road, Glenfield, Auckland 0627, New Zealand
A 53, Sector 57, Noida, UP, India
77–85 Fulham Palace Road, London W6 8JB, United Kingdom
2 Bloor Street East, 20th floor, Toronto, Ontario M4W 1A8, Canada
10 East 53rd Street, New York NY 10022, USA

National Library of Australia Cataloguing-in-Publication entry:

Warren, Katrina.
Wonderdogs tricks and training / Katrina Warren,
Kelly Gill.
ISBN:9780732294793 (pbk.)
Dogs – Training.
Other Authors/Contributors: Gill, Kelly.

636.70835

Cover design by Christabella Designs
Cover image by James Morgan
Internal studio photographs by James Morgan
Internal design by Christabella Designs
Typeset in Avenir 55 Roman by Christabella Designs
Colour reproduction by Graphic Print Group, Adelaide
Printed and bound in China by RR Donnelley on 128gsm matt art